PARIS

GILL STACEY

WORLD ALMANAC® LIBRARY

Please visit our web site at: www.worldalmanaclibrary.com
For a free color catalog describing World Almanac® Library's list of high-quality books
and multimedia programs, call 1-800-848-2928 (USA) or 1-800-387-3178 (Canada).
World Almanac® Library's fax: (414) 332-3567.

Library of Congress Cataloging-in-Publication Data available upon request from publisher.
Fax (414) 336-0157 for the attention of the Publishing Records Department.

ISBN 0-8368-5030-0 (lib. bdg.)
ISBN 0-8368-5190-0 (softcover)

First published in 2004 by
World Almanac® Library
330 West Olive Street, Suite 100
Milwaukee, WI 53212 USA

Copyright © 2004 by World Almanac® Library.

Produced by Discovery Books
Editor: Kathryn Walker
Series designers: Laurie Shock, Keith Williams
Designer and page production: Rob Norridge
Photo researcher: Rachel Tisdale
Maps: Stefan Chabluk
World Almanac® Library editorial direction: Mark J. Sachner
World Almanac® Library editor: Jenette Donovan Guntly
World Almanac® Library art direction: Tammy Gruenewald
World Almanac® Library production: Jessica Morris

Photo credits: AKG-Images: pp.11, 12, 14, 15; AKG-Images/Archives CDA/Guillot: p. 22; AKG-Images/Jerome da
Cunha: p. 10; AKG-Images/Joseph Martin: 30; AKG-Images/Schützel/Rodemann: pp. 24, 32; Art Directors & Trip/T.
Bognar: 28; Chris Fairclough Photography: pp. 16, 17, 23, 25, 38, 40; CORBIS: cover and title page, pp. 4, 9, 13, 41;
CORBIS/Stephanie Cardinale/People Avenue: p. 33; CORBIS/Robert Holmes: 27; CORBIS/Charles & Josette Lonmas:
p. 21; CORBIS SUGMA/Pitchal Frederic: p. 42; David Simson – DASPHOTOGB@aol.com: p. 37; Eye Ubiquitous/Brian
Harding: 39; Eye Ubiquitous/Andy Hibbert: p. 31; Hutchison/Bernard Rogent: 29; James Davis Travel Photography:
p. 35; Mary Evans Picture Library: p. 8; Still Pictures/Nigel Dickinson: pp. 18, 19, 36; Trip/ASK Images: p. 20

Cover caption: Originally intended as a temporary structure, the Eiffel Tower has become a symbol of Paris.

Printed in the United States of America

1 2 3 4 5 6 7 8 9 08 07 06 05 04

Contents

Introduction

Paris is the capital city of France. It lies in northern France on the right (north) and left (south) banks of the Seine River.

When people refer to Paris, they usually mean the city of Paris. Stretching out beyond the city are the suburbs of Paris, known as the *banlieues*. The city, the suburbs, and the surrounding satellite towns and countryside make up the administrative region known as the Ile de France, of which Paris is also the capital.

◀ *The Eiffel Tower, the famous symbol of Paris, dominates the city skyline.*

A Romantic City

Paris is often described as the most romantic city in the world. Its different features have a unique appeal: the Seine and its many bridges, the wide boulevards, the beautiful buildings, and the striking monuments. The various districts, known as the *arrondissements*, each have their own special character, from the upscale 8th arrondissement surrounding the Champs Elysées (one of the city's grandest boulevards), to the vibrant, multicultural 20th arrondissement.

Many people consider Paris to be the cultural capital of Europe and it is sometimes known as the "city of light" because of its special place as a center of learning. Many famous painters, writers, and philosophers have lived in Paris, among them Pablo Picasso, Claude Monet, Ernest Hemingway, and Jean-Paul Sartre.

Power Base

Paris is the seat of France's government. The French Parliament is divided into two bodies — the National Assembly, which meets at the Bourbon Palace, and the Senate, which meets at the Luxembourg Palace. The Elysée Palace, near the Champs Elysées, is the residence of the president of France.

Paris and the surrounding Ile de France region are also the "powerhouse" of France: about 25 percent of the French workforce is based there. The city is home to many leading French and international businesses, while important manufacturing industries are based in the suburbs and satellite towns.

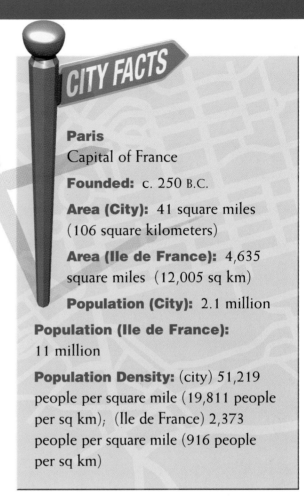

CITY FACTS

Paris
Capital of France

Founded: c. 250 B.C.

Area (City): 41 square miles (106 square kilometers)

Area (Ile de France): 4,635 square miles (12,005 sq km)

Population (City): 2.1 million

Population (Ile de France): 11 million

Population Density: (city) 51,219 people per square mile (19,811 people per sq km); (Ile de France) 2,373 people per square mile (916 people per sq km)

A Modern City

Paris is rich in history and culture, but it is also a dynamic, modern city that looks to the future with bold architectural designs, such as the Pompidou Center (an arts and cultural center) and futuristic city developments, like that of La Défense, the new business district on the city's western outskirts.

"If you are lucky enough to have lived in Paris as a young man, then wherever you go for the rest of your life, it stays with you, for Paris is a moveable feast."

—Ernest Hemingway, *A Moveable Feast*, 1964.

Ile de France

▲ *The Ile de France is divided into eight departments. The suburbs of Paris, the darker shaded area around the city, extend into three of them.*

Geography

Paris is situated in the Paris Basin, a large plain through which the Seine has cut wide valleys. The historic city of Paris occupies a bowl created by the Seine, with its perimeter defined by areas of higher land around it.

The city is divided into twenty numbered arrondissements. Most of these are north of the Seine, in an area known as the Right Bank. Traditionally, the Right Bank has been associated with business, fashion, and entertainment, while the Left Bank (the south side of the river) has been the domain of artists, intellectuals, and students. Running around the edge of the city today is a beltway, the Périphérique, and beyond this lie the suburbs.

The Seine River

The Seine lies at the heart of Paris. It has been used to transport goods since the Romans first arrived more than two thousand years ago, and Paris built much of its early wealth from this trade. The historic center of Paris is the small island in the Seine called the Ile de la Cité (Isle of the City), where the region's earliest inhabitants settled. Upstream is the smaller Ile Saint-Louis, today an expensive residential area with fine, old houses and narrow streets. Alongside much of the river, below street level, are tree-lined quays where people can walk, picnic, and sometimes go fishing.

There are more than thirty bridges crossing the Seine in Paris. The most famous and oldest is, ironically, the Pont Neuf (New Bridge), which dates from the sixteenth century. The Pont des Arts, a two-hundred-year-old iron pedestrian bridge, has probably the finest views over the river.

Paris Arrondissements

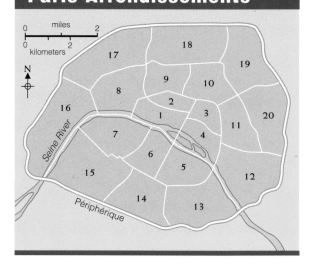

Paris City Center

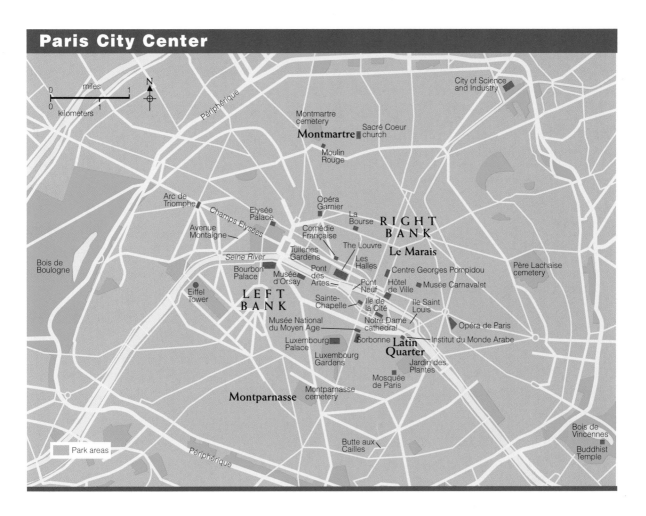

On the Right Bank are many of the city's most famous monuments and buildings. Radiating out from the Arc de Triomphe, the huge triumphal arch built by Napoleon I, are twelve wide and elegant boulevards. To the east, near the river, is the Louvre Museum and the Pompidou Center; to the north, at the highest point of Paris, lies a section of the city called Montmartre.

On the Left Bank is the Sorbonne, the most famous part of the University of Paris, in the lively Latin Quarter; and the city's most striking landmark, the Eiffel Tower.

Climate

Paris has four distinct seasons. In spring (March through May), the weather is mild and many believe this to be the time when the city is most beautiful. Summers are usually warm and can be hot, especially in July and August, when the average maximum temperature is 75° Fahrenheit (24° Celsius). Fall (September through November) is cool, and winter can be cold, with temperatures that can drop as low as −1° F (−18° C). Rainfall is usually spread across all four seasons.

CHAPTER 1

History of Paris

The people who first settled in what is today the heart of Paris — the island of the Ile de la Cité — were the Parisii. A Celtic tribe, they chose this small island in the Seine because of its good fishing, fertile land, and its surrounding hills, which formed a natural defense against attack. They established their settlement in about 250 B.C.

In 52 B.C., the Parisii settlement was conquered by the Romans, led by Julius Caesar, and was named Lutetia. The town grew and became an important center for the Roman Empire. In the third century A.D., Lutetia was officially renamed Paris, for its early settlers. By this time, Christianity had been introduced to the city.

End of Roman Rule

By the beginning of the fifth century, the power of the Roman Empire was weakening, and Roman rule had virtually come to an end. Attacks by the Huns, a fierce, nomadic tribe from Asia, and by other barbarian tribes threatened to destroy Paris. At the end of the fifth century, a Germanic tribe known as the Franks took control of Paris. In 508, their leader, Clovis, made Paris his capital and founded the Merovingian dynasty. In the eighth century, a new

◀ *A medieval painting shows peasants in the fifteenth century sowing seeds in the fields around the Louvre fortress.*

dynasty, the Carolingians, took control; they moved their capital away from Paris to Aix-la-Chapelle (now Aachen in Germany), and Paris went into decline.

The Capetians

In 987, Hugh Capet, count of Paris, was crowned King of France, and Paris again became the French capital. Between the tenth and fourteenth centuries, Paris began to grow in size and power once more, this time under the Capetian dynasty. The Louvre (now a world-famous museum, but constructed originally as a fortress) and the grand Notre Dame Cathedral were built. The city became a great center of learning, leading to the establishment of the University of Paris in 1253.

War with England

There were troubled times in the fourteenth and fifteenth centuries under the Valois dynasty. The Hundred Years' War between England and France (1337–1453) greatly weakened the French monarchy and destabilized France — and also its capital. A terrible plague, known as the Black Death, hit Paris in 1348, killing thousands of Parisians. Paris fell briefly under English rule between 1419 and 1436. By the end of the Hundred Years' War, the city had lost half its population.

The Renaissance

Toward the end of the fifteenth century and during the sixteenth century, the fortunes of Paris revived and its population began to grow again. Printing was introduced and more Parisians were able to buy and read books. Royal power and wealth increased, especially under Francis I (1515–1547), a Valois and the first of the French Renaissance kings. The Renaissance was a great cultural movement that started in Italy in the fourteenth century, characterized by a revival of interest in ancient Greek and Roman learning, art, and architecture. Francis encouraged new styles in French architecture that were influenced by the Italian Renaissance, with elegant columns, decorated ceilings and statues. The Hôtel

◄ The Notre Dame Cathedral was founded in the twelfth century. It stands on the east end of the Ile de la Cité, at the geographical center of Paris.

de Ville (Town Hall) was rebuilt in the Renaissance style, and the Louvre fortress was transformed into a Renaissance palace.

Wars of Religion

In the sixteenth century, religious conflict raged across Europe. In Paris, the Roman Catholics, who were in the majority, fought the Protestant Huguenots in the Wars of Religion (1562–1598). The most infamous incident of these wars occurred on St. Bartholomew's Day, August 24, 1572, when Catholics took part in a massacre of thousands of Huguenots in Paris.

The wars came to an end under Henry IV, the first of the Bourbon dynasty. Henry had to convert to Catholicism before Paris would accept him and he could become king, but once in power, he granted freedom of worship throughout France. After many

▼ *The Hall of Mirrors at Versailles — the palace built by the "Sun KIng" to reflect the power of the monarchy.*

attempts on his life, he was assassinated by a Catholic fanatic in 1610.

The Sun King

It was under Louis XIV (1643–1715) that the Bourbon kings became all powerful. Louis, known as the "Sun King," moved the French court out of the city to nearby Versailles, about 14 miles (23 km) southwest of Paris. During his reign, there were great cultural achievements in music, drama, and art. Two of France's most famous playwrights, Molière and Jean Racine, wrote at this time. Louis also waged wars against other European countries; his lavish spending combined with these costly wars nearly bankrupted France.

Growing Discontent

By the eighteenth century, the Bourbon dynasty had become weak, corrupt, and even more extravagant. Expensive wars continued to be fought against European rivals. Meanwhile, the majority of Parisians lived in great poverty. The unpopularity of the Bourbons reached its height during the reign of Louis XVI and his wife, Marie Antoinette, from 1774 to1792.

The population of Paris continued to grow and new industries developed, particularly in the suburbs. The social order was changing and the ideas of a new movement, the Enlightenment, were causing people to question old values. Writers and philosophers of the Enlightenment, many of them from Paris, believed that society

▲ *Crowds gathered at the Place de la Révolution (now known as the Place de la Concorde) to watch the execution of King Louis XVI on January 21, 1793.*

should be based on rational thought and science rather than on traditional forms of government and religion. Parisians, influenced by these ideas, were beginning to challenge royal authority and religion.

Popular feeling against the monarchy reached the boiling point when, in the 1780s, the Paris authorities decided to tax all trade goods that came into Paris. They built a toll wall with more than fifty toll houses, or collection points, to make sure the taxes were paid. In 1788, failed harvests caused great hardship for the poor and led to rioting.

The French Revolution

The act that began the French Revolution was the storming of the Bastille Prison on July 14, 1789, by a Parisian mob. They also attacked the hated toll wall — like the Bastille, it was a symbol of injustice and repression for the ordinary people. Paris was at the heart of the revolution that followed.

The revolution saw the violent overthrow of the monarchy that had ruled France for hundreds of years. People wanted a new type of government that was just and would help them to break free from poverty. In the first hopeful months of the revolution, there was a new government, new laws, debates, and the proclamation of high ideals about the "rights of man."

▶ *Portrait of Emperor Napoleon I in his coronation robes. He crowned himself emperor in 1804.*

In 1792, the monarchy was officially abolished and the First Republic was declared. Revolutionaries Georges Jacques Danton, Jean-Paul Marat, and Maximilien Robespierre took control. The democratic ideals and free political debate of the first days of the revolution were soon replaced by the Reign of Terror, between 1793 and 1794, a period of near mob rule when there was no government or army control. Armed gangs roamed the streets of Paris, and many ordinary citizens lived in fear for their lives. Any suspected opponents of the revolution were rounded up, and thousands were publicly executed by guillotine, including the king and queen in 1793.

A New Empire

Amid this chaos, Napoleon Bonaparte, a Corsican soldier, seized power in 1799, and in 1804, he declared himself emperor of France. His ambitions for the new empire led to wars of expansion across Europe and eventually to his downfall. He died in exile in 1821.

"Even when I am gone, I shall remain in people's minds the star of their rights, my name will be the war cry of their efforts, the motto of their hopes."

—Napoleon Bonaparte, emperor of France.

Napoleon's legacy for France, and for Paris in particular, lay in a new legal system (Code Napoleon), in education, and in building. He centralized France and the French empire around Paris, ensuring that political power and important political decisions always came from the capital. He enriched the city with works of art captured during wars of conquest and had grand monuments built to glorify his name, such as the Arc de Triomphe and the column in the Place Vendôme, both celebrating his brilliant military victory at Austerlitz in 1805.

After Napoleon

In 1815, the monarchy was restored, but weak and repressive kings met opposition from the growing working class as the industrial revolution (great changes brought about by the introduction of machinery in industry) spread in Paris and to the rest of France. The unpopularity of the French kings resulted in the revolutions of 1830 and 1848, when the two reigning monarchs were overthrown. These revolutions were, once again, led by Parisians.

In 1848, France became a republic once more. Louis-Napoleon was elected as president of the Second Republic; then declared himself Emperor Napoleon III. During his time, Paris was transformed into the city that we see today. This was mainly through the building and development directed by Baron Georges Eugène Haussmann, the administrator appointed to carry out Louis-Napoleon's grand plans for making Paris an impressive modern city. However, a crushing defeat in 1870, during a war with the powerful north German kingdom of Prussia, forced Napoleon III to abdicate.

Between 1870 and 1871, the city was besieged, and then briefly occupied, by the Prussians. After their withdrawal, Parisian workers took control of the city and established the Paris Commune, a radical form of government led by poor, working people. The Commune was over within weeks, ruthlessly suppressed by the French army, and the Third Republic began.

The Eiffel Tower

The Eiffel Tower (above) is the most famous — and the most visited — monument in Paris. It was built for the Paris World's Fair in 1889 (and was intended to be taken down afterward). Its designer, Gustave Eiffel, wanted to create the tallest monument in the world. To do so, he used iron girders so that the tower would be lighter than a solid brick structure and would be able to rise higher. It soars to more than 1,000 feet (305 m), offering fantastic views over the city. At the time it was built, the Eiffel Tower was controversial: Some Parisians loved it. Others hated it.

In the last years of the nineteenth century, Paris changed quickly. The population was growing; new railroads and the Métro (the Parisian subway system) were built. Many new buildings, including the Eiffel Tower, were erected. The *Belle Époque* (Beautiful Age) began, a period famed for the flowing lines of its distinctive Art Nouveau architecture and for advances in science and the arts.

The Two World Wars

For the first years of the twentieth century, the Belle Époque continued to flourish. But World War I (1914–1918) brought terrible suffering to France, and more than 1 million French soldiers were killed. German forces attempted to terrorize Parisians into submission by shelling the city with a massive gun known as "Big Bertha," but they did not manage to capture Paris. In 1919,

the Treaty of Versailles, the peace treaty that officially ended World War I, was negotiated at Versailles and signed in the palace's Hall of Mirrors.

In the 1930s, the severe economic crisis known as the Great Depression spread from the United States to Europe. In Paris as elsewhere, businesses collapsed causing unemployment, yet the city remained a great intellectual and cultural center. It continued to attract writers and artists from all around the world.

In 1940, during World War II (from 1939 to 1945), Paris was captured by the Germans. The French government and many thousands of Parisians fled the city. The Nazi symbol, the swastika, hung above many of Paris's most beloved buildings, including the Hôtel de Ville and the Eiffel Tower. Four years of occupation and oppression followed. Many Parisians joined secret resistance movements to fight the Germans, and the Free French Army, made up of exiled troops, was formed.

The city was finally liberated by the British, Canadian, and American Allied Forces, and the Free French Army, in 1944. The leader of the Free French, Charles de Gaulle, became president for a brief period. After the war, the rebuilding of a shattered nation was heralded with a new constitution and the beginning of the Fourth Republic.

Modern Paris

The Fifth Republic began in 1958 when de Gaulle once again became president. In 1968, student and worker unrest and strikes nearly brought down the government, and de Gaulle resigned.

The 1970s and 1980s saw much redevelopment and modernization in Paris, under the presidencies of Georges Pompidou and François Mitterrand. In particular, it was the "grand projects" of Mitterrand (France's first socialist president) that transformed parts of the city. Huge sums of money were invested in these grand projects — modern, often futuristic architecture, which included the controversial glass pyramid at the Louvre; the new opera house at the Place de la Bastille (where the prison once stood); the Grande Arche de la Défense; and the Institute of the Arab World.

In 1975, the powerful post of mayor of Paris was created. Jacques Chirac, a conservative, was elected mayor in 1977, a position he held until 1995. Over the years, Chirac built up his power base and influence. He was elected president in 1995 and again in 2002.

▼ *Possibly the most famous of Mitterrand's "grand projects" involved the addition of a glass pyramid over the new underground entrance to the Louvre.*

CHAPTER 2

People of Paris

The majority of Parisians were born in France and have French parents and grandparents. Many have lived in the city for generations and think of themselves first and foremost as Parisians. Others come perhaps for just a few years to work or to study.

Paris is also a multicultural city — immigrants and refugees have come to settle there over several hundred years, and their presence has helped shape contemporary Parisian culture. Today, about one-fifth of Paris's residents are immigrants, mostly from former French colonies (countries once ruled by France). Many have settled in the poorer areas of the city, such as the 3rd, 5th, 19th, and 20th arrondissements, where housing is cheaper. There are also large immigrant communities in the suburbs of Paris.

Different Communities and Cultures

Among the African and Caribbean communities of Paris, the largest number of residents came originally from the French colonies of North Africa — mainly Algeria, but also Tunisia and Morocco. There are also Africans from France's former West African colonies, such as Mali, Senegal, and the Ivory Coast. A smaller number of residents have come from the Caribbean colonies of Haiti and Martinique.

◄ *Cafés are an important part of Parisian life; they are places where people socialize throughout the day.*

Immigrants from the former colony of Indochina (Cambodia, Vietnam, and Laos) make up the Southeast Asian communities of Paris. The majority live in the area known as Chinatown in the 13th arrondissement.

Other Europeans

People from other countries of the European Union and elsewhere in Europe often come to live in Paris. Most stay only a few years, but some have made the city their home. In the 1950s and 1960s, many families left Portugal and Spain — countries which were then both poor and undemocratic — in search of a better life in Paris. The majority of this group has remained in Paris. Since the fall of communism in Russia and Eastern

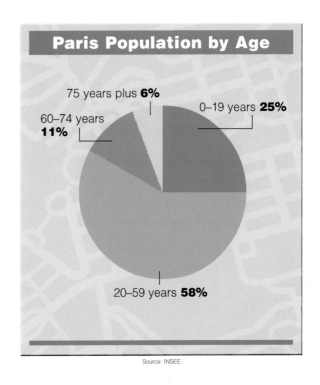

Paris Population by Age

75 years plus **6%**

60–74 years **11%**

0–19 years **25%**

20–59 years **58%**

Source: INSEE

Jewish Parisians

The Jewish community is the oldest immigrant community in Paris — there have been Jewish communities in the city since the sixth century. Throughout history, Parisian Jews have been terribly persecuted, but never more so than during the Nazi occupation of Paris during World War II, when thousands were rounded up and sent to their deaths in concentration camps. The Jewish community has survived and grown in numbers with the arrival of Jewish migrants from North Africa in the 1960s. Today, there are more than 300,000 Jews and many synagogues in the city and suburbs of Paris. The heart of the Jewish community is in the Marais area (right) in the 3rd arrondissement.

Europe, a similar pattern has emerged, with families arriving from countries such as Poland and Romania.

Racial Tensions

Many of the children and grandchildren of earlier immigrants now have French nationality and think of themselves as Parisians. But, as the number of different nationalities in Paris has grown, so too has tension between ethnic groups. Recent anti-immigration policies and the poor housing endured by many African and Southeast Asian communities have made matters worse. The problem is at its most visible in the run-down public housing developments in the poorer parts of the Paris suburbs.

A Changing Population

It is not just the arrival of immigrants that is changing the population structure of Paris. In recent years, different areas within the city of Paris have been redeveloped, making them more expensive places to live. Traditional Parisian communities are being broken up, as families have moved out to less expensive homes in the suburbs and new satellite towns around Paris.

Religion

The main religious faith in Paris is Christianity. Most French Christians belong to the Roman Catholic Church, with a much smaller number belonging to one of fifteen Protestant churches. Since the French Revolution, church and state have been completely separate, and there is no religious teaching in schools. In France, religious faith is very much a personal matter.

Catholicism

There are many Catholic churches in Paris, the most famous of them being the great gothic Notre Dame Cathedral on the Ile de la Cité. Other Paris churches renowned for their beauty are the thirteenth-century Sainte-Chapelle, also on the Ile de la Cité; and the white-domed Sacré-Coeur Basilica in Montmartre, dating from the nineteenth

◀ *The Sacré-Coeur (Sacred Heart) Basilica sits atop the hill of Montmartre and offers visitors some of the best panoramic views of Paris.*

century. In recent years, the numbers of practicing Catholics has declined, especially among the young. Nearly half of young French people today claim to have no religion. Yet, when the Pope came to Paris in 1997 for a World Youth Day, about 1 million French youths came to hear him.

Islam

After Christianity, the most widely followed religion in Paris is Islam. Most of Paris's African community (from both North and West Africa) are Muslims, but there are also practicing Muslims among the Turkish and Asian communities. Paris has about one hundred mosques, where Muslims go to pray and to study the Koran (the Islamic holy book) and Islamic law. The Mosquée de Paris (Paris Mosque) was built in 1926 in the Latin Quarter. It is the oldest mosque in France and is the center of the country's Muslim community. Near the mosque is the Institut du Monde Arabe (Institute of the Arab World), which was opened in 1987 as a cultural center to help develop understanding of the Arab world.

Buddhism

The Buddhist religion is growing in popularity in Paris — and in France as a whole — especially among people under fifty. In the *Bois de Vincennes* (Woods of Vincennes), a park at the southeastern edge of the city, sits the Buddhist Center and the Buddhist Temple of Paris.

▲ The Paris Mosque, in the Latin Quarter, was built in the 1920s in honor of the North African Muslims who aided France during World War I.

Celebrations and Festivals

Paris has many festivals and celebrations throughout the year, but the most important of them all is Bastille Day. Celebrated every year on July 14, it commemorates the storming of the Bastille Prison in 1789. For Parisians especially, it symbolizes the overthrow of the privileged, corrupt monarchy and aristocracy during the French Revolution and the birth of the French

▲ Thousands attend an open-air concert at the Place Vendôme, part of the daylong Fête de la Musique celebrations held throughout the city every June 21.

Republic. Bastille Day is a day of constant partying, with street fairs, balls, feasting at home or in bars and restaurants, and dancing in the streets. There is a huge parade along the Champs Elysées and fireworks displays in the evening.

Paris also has many wonderful music festivals. On the longest day of the year, June 21, the unique Fête de la Musique is held. For the whole day, Paris becomes a city of free music. Musicians ranging from unknown street musicians to world-famous stars perform on street corners, at cafés, and in large concert venues.

Later in the year, the autumn festival of theater, music, and dance — the Festival d'Automne — begins in mid-September and continues until the end of December. Performances take place in museums and churches throughout the city. The short, dreary days of December are lit up by Africolor, a music festival held in the suburb of Saint-Denis to celebrate the different cultures of Paris's African communities.

Celebrations of the produce of autumn are reflected in two smaller October festivals: During the Salon de Champignons, people go out to collect wild mushrooms from the forests around Paris; the Fêtes des Vendanges is held when the last grapes of the season are harvested in Montmartre.

For Parisians, Christmas celebrations are centered mostly on family. On the evening of December 24, many families share a special Christmas meal and then attend Midnight Mass at their local church or at Notre Dame Cathedral.

Dining Out

Parisians love food and they love to dine out. The city has long been famous for its restaurants. They range from the elegant, exclusive, and very expensive restaurants, often run by acclaimed chefs, to the smaller, often family-run places, known as *bistros*. Bistros mostly offer hearty regional food at reasonable prices. There are also *brasseries* — larger restaurants that are open all day serving meals and snacks or just drinks. Paris is famous for its café life. People meet at cafés to sip strong black

▼ At the end of January or early February, celebrations take place to mark the Chinese New Year. Colorful lions make their way along the narrow streets of Chinatown in the 13th arrondissement.

"Everything ends this way in France — evenings, weddings, christenings, duels, burials, swindlings, diplomatic affairs — everything is a pretext for a good dinner."

—Jean Anouilh, French playwright.

coffee, drink wine or beer, and eat snacks. Cafés are also great places for lively discussion and people watching.

French cuisine is not the only type of food available in the city — there are many inexpensive ethnic eating places. The widest choice is probably found in the 11th and 13th arrondissements, where Vietnamese,

▼ *The Restaurant Pharamond in the posh 1st arrondissement has a typically Art Nouveau interior.*

Chinese, Thai, and North African restaurants offer foods from around the world. Specialties of North African restaurants include couscous, a type of millet that is steamed and served with a spicy stew, sweet pastries, and refreshing mint tea.

Eating at Home

Whether they are eating at home or dining out, Parisians look for the best quality in their food. People often buy from small stores and open-air markets, rather than supermarkets. On almost all Paris streets, there are specialty shops with beautifully presented displays of food: *boulangeries* (bakeries), which sell freshly baked bread; *pâtisseries* (pastry shops), where there are tempting rich cakes or tarts to buy; and *charcuteries*, shops that sell cold meats. Most neighborhoods also have their own street food markets, offering a huge selection of the freshest seasonal fruits and vegetables.

A family meal, especially on weekends or for special occasions, will often have several courses. It might start with crudités (fresh, finely sliced raw vegetables), cold meats, or soup. The main course is often meat. A meal may end with cheese, a dessert, or fresh fruit. Parisians love rich, often strong-tasting cheeses, such as Normandy Camembert from northwest France or Roquefort, a blue cheese made from sheep's milk, from the southwest region. People will often buy dessert from a pâtisserie — especially popular are tarts made with fresh fruit, such as *tarte aux pommes* (apple tart).

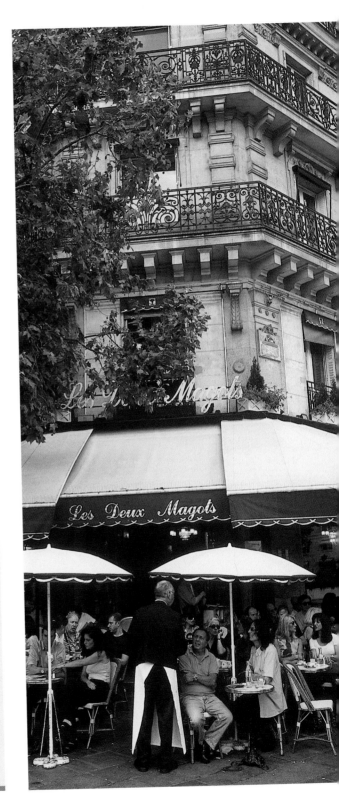

▶ *The popular Deux Magots café on the Left Bank was a regular meeting place for many well-known writers and artists during the 1920s and 1930s.*

Tradition and Change

Parisians have often been regarded as food snobs, who reject any notion of fast food. But in recent years, many Parisians, especially the young, have begun to change their attitude toward food. Restaurant chains and fast-food restaurants have sprung up all over the city, especially in the areas popular with tourists. Small, family-owned restaurants find it hard to compete, and many have closed down. Changing patterns of work are leading to changes in eating habits as well. Lunch is no longer the main meal of the day — people may eat a sandwich, a salad, or a quick carryout meal instead of a large meal.

The Baguette

For the traditionalist, the fall in demand for the baguette is symbolic of the decline of French eating habits. The baguette is a long, thin, crusty loaf of white bread that is bought freshly baked — several batches are often baked each day — and has long been seen as an essential accompaniment to almost every meal. The baguette goes stale very quickly and has to be eaten on the day it is purchased. Today, many Parisians are turning either to cheaper, mass-produced bread, which keeps longer, or to healthful, whole wheat bread.

CHAPTER 3

Living in Paris

Most Parisians live in apartments, though a wealthy few may live in houses. Apartments are often small with little space for families, especially in poorer areas. It is rare to have a yard in Paris, but quite a few apartment buildings have courtyards or balconies. The majority of Parisians rent rather than buy their homes, although an increasing number of people are seeking to buy their homes today — if they can afford them.

Types of Housing

Many of the homes in the city of Paris date from the nineteenth and early twentieth centuries. In the mid-nineteenth century, the city was transformed by Baron Haussmann. He gave the city much of the look that it has today: the geometric design, the wide boulevards, and the elegant apartment buildings with wrought-iron balcony railings. New apartment buildings and houses were built during the twentieth century, especially after World War II. The rebuilding and modernization projects led to the demolition of many of Paris's old, narrow streets as well as its slums. Today, there are just a few high-rise buildings in the city of Paris.

◀ *Traditional Parisian apartments alongside the Seine often have balconies with wrought-iron railings and shuttered windows.*

The Parisian Concierge

Until recent years, the concierge has always been a unique feature of Paris apartment buildings. The concierge is someone who, in return for accommodations, cleans and maintains the building, distributes the mail, and generally watches over the place. In the 1950s and 1960s, French concierges were largely replaced by Spanish and Portuguese immigrants, who squeezed their families into tiny lodgings on the ground floor of the building. Today, many of these concierges are retiring. Younger people want better-paying jobs and more spacious accommodations. The human face of the concierge is being replaced by security systems, intercoms, and elevators in many buildings.

" … good concierges [apartment managers] are getting hard to find these days. Few people are prepared to live in a dark and cramped ground-floor lodge, at the beck and call of every resident."

—Jon Henley, journalist, 2002.

has become very overcrowded, causing the city authorities to place restrictions on the number of people moving into the area.

Living in the Suburbs

About 75 percent of all Parisians now live in the suburbs, or banlieues, which were

▼ *This modern housing development is one of several in the Belleville area, in the northeast part of the city.*

The housing in each arrondissement often has its own special character. The Marais area in the 3rd arrondissement has many grand houses, known as *hôtels*, that date from the seventeenth century. Once a very wealthy area where the aristocracy lived, the Marais began to decline in the eighteenth century. Now, it is once again a fashionable area, and property prices there have soared. In the 13th arrondissement, on the Left Bank, the old houses and cobblestone streets of the traditionally working-class area of Butte aux Cailles contrast with the modern high-rise buildings of nearby Chinatown and the new developments of the 1990s. Housing there developed after World War II to accommodate workers both from Paris and from the nearby industrial areas. The low cost of housing meant that they also became home to newly arrived and often poor immigrant communities.

Life in the suburbs is somewhat different from life in the city of Paris. Those with more money tend to live in the more desirable, spacious suburbs, such as Neuilly, Boulogne, and Vincennes, where there are large houses with yards, good local schools, and other facilities. Life is quieter and usually more family-centered there than in the city.

Other suburbs, especially to the north of Paris, are poorer and more deprived. In suburbs such as Sarcelles, families are housed in large developments of grim high-rise apartment buildings, with few local facilities.

Montreuil

On the eastern edge of the city of Paris is the town of Montreuil. It is a working-class town of about 100,000 inhabitants, with large North and West African communities and many languages spoken in the town's schools. Yet Montreuil has small-scale, inexpensive housing and excellent facilities for all, such as schools, libraries, and green spaces. It has few of the social or racial problems of the poor northern suburbs. In recent years, Montreuil has attracted many young families, who can live in pleasant apartments that are less costly and more spacious than anywhere in central Paris.

These conditions have led to many social problems, including high rates of crime, drug abuse, and vandalism, especially among bored and discontented young people.

Homelessness

The problem of homelessness in Paris has increased alarmingly in recent years. With unemployment rising since the 1980s, there is a growing divide — especially in the city — between the wealthy and the poor. It is difficult to estimate exactly how many thousands sleep on the streets of Paris every night, but the number has increased in recent years, largely due to several thousand destitute asylum-seekers from Afghanistan, the former Yugoslavia, and countries in Africa.

Education for Children

Working parents in Paris can put their children into government-run *crèches*, or nurseries, from the age of three months. Most young children start preschool, or kindergarten, at age three. They then start elementary school at six, moving on to junior high school at eleven. At fifteen, they move up to high school, known as *lycée*.

Education is compulsory until age sixteen. Most children attend public schools, which provide free education, but a minority go to private schools in Paris, which are often run by the Catholic Church. Children who stay on in full-time education after the age of sixteen study a range of different subjects in order to earn

▲ *A class of schoolchildren gathers in front of a painting by Henri Matisse on a visit to the National Museum of Modern Art in the Pompidou Center.*

their diploma, known as a *baccalauréat*. Passing the "bac" guarantees a student a place at a university. It is also a necessary qualification for top-level jobs.

Educational Issues

The French are proud of their nation's educational achievements, but problems within the system are growing. This is particularly true in Paris, where more pupils are leaving school with no qualifications. An increasing number are leaving with poor levels of ability in reading, writing, and math. Violence in schools is also on the rise.

Higher Education

One in four of all French college students attends the University of Paris. The university was founded 750 years ago and later divided into several different colleges, including the world-famous Sorbonne. The international reputation of the university has long attracted leading academics, both to teach and to carry out research. These include the scientists Pierre and Marie Curie, whose research into radiation revolutionized modern medicine.

However, the numbers of students at the university are very high and this has led to little personal contact between students and their professors. Students have long

Les Grandes Écoles

The grande écoles are schools of higher education for students who want to specialize in subjects such as business administration, engineering, and management. Before entering a grande école, students must take two to three years of special post-baccalauréat classes. Graduates of these schools often go to the top of their chosen professions. One of the most prestigious is the École Polytechnique, founded by Emperor Napoleon I to train engineers for the armed forces.

▲ *The Place de la Sorbonne, in front of the University of Paris church, is a popular student meeting place.*

complained about the old-fashioned and formal styles of teaching at the university. In 1968, radical students rebelled, joining striking workers on the streets of Paris in protests against the "establishment" — the government, the workplace, and the education system.

After 1968, the university was divided into several smaller faculties, which are spread out across the city of Paris and the suburbs. Today's students are less rebellious than their predecessors of the 1960s. In an era of high unemployment, most work hard, seeing their time in college as a stepping stone to a good career. Yet Paris's students still frequent cafés and bars, endlessly debating and philosophizing.

Paris also has specialized institutes and colleges, including the French Institute, which is made up of five academies; and the Pasteur Institute for medical research.

Several prestigious business schools are also based in or near Paris.

Shopping

For those who love to shop, whether they are residents or visitors, Paris is a special experience. There are shops and markets to cater to all tastes and all budgets.

The city has several large department stores, including the Samaritaine, Galeries Lafayette, Au Printemps, Au Bon Marché, and Monoprix. There are also shopping malls, such as the huge complex at Les Halles, a multilevel underground complex on the Right Bank that has more than 180 different stores. Those looking for a bargain can explore the "flea markets," which sell everything from antiques to cheap bric-a-brac. The largest is the Marché aux Puces de Clignancourt in the 18th arrondissement, which has over two thousand different stalls.

When it comes to fashion, the different districts often have their own flavor and feel. Wealthy shoppers buy expensive *haute couture* (high fashion) clothing from the exclusive shops and fashion houses in the 1st and 8th arrondissements. On the elegant Avenue Montaigne are famous designer names, including Calvin Klein, Christian Dior, and Dolce e Gabbana.

Shoppers on tighter budgets, who seek that essential Parisian *"chic"* (a way of dressing that is elegant, yet seems effortless), search out the many boutiques across the city. These stylish small shops sell the latest fashions in a wide range of prices.

The Passages

Among the smaller, more unusual places to shop in Paris are the covered passages (above). They opened in the early nineteenth century to allow wealthy people to shop safely, away from the dirt and noise of the open streets. Many have been closed or demolished, but several have recently been restored, including the oldest — Passage du Caire. The passages are known for their mix of interesting specialty shops.

▲ *The entrance to the Porte-Dauphine Métro station is in the Art Nouveau style that typified the period about a century ago known as the Belle Époque.*

Getting Around

Like most major European cities, Paris suffers from serious road traffic problems. However, by contrast with many of them, Paris's public transportation system is efficient, clean, and inexpensive. Many Parisians travel to work using the subway trains, the railroad system, or the buses. People from the outer suburbs or satellite towns may spend more than an hour each way commuting to their workplaces.

The Métro

The subway system in Paris is known as the Métro. In all, there are fourteen different lines that crisscross the city. The first Métro line opened just over one hundred years ago, and today, it is one of the most modern, efficient underground systems in the world. With more than 360 stations, it is said that every building in Paris is within about 500 yards (457 meters) of a Métro station.

Railroad Links

Paris has six main stations with railroad lines to all parts of France and the rest of Europe. High-speed trains called TGVs (TGV stands for *"Train à Grande Vitesse,"* which means "high-speed train") depart from Paris to most parts of France and other countries in Europe. Eurostar trains link Paris with London and Brussels. A regional network of express trains, known as the RER, transports workers to and from the suburbs into the center of Paris.

Air and Road

Paris has two major airports. Charles de Gaulle, 14 miles (23 km) north of Paris, is the larger airport and handles most international flights. Orly Airport, 10 miles (16 km) south of the city, is for domestic and short-distance international flights.

The many narrow streets in the city and the increase in car traffic have made Paris's roads more crowded than ever. In spite of this, many commuters choose to drive to work, creating serious traffic jams during the morning and evening rush hours. As a result, air pollution in Paris is worsening. In the 1970s, a new beltway, the Périphérique, was built to carry heavy traffic in and around Paris. This too has become congested in recent years.

The French are passionate cyclists, and in recent years, the city authorities have created many miles of bicycle lanes across the city. Yet, with the crowded streets and the speed of the traffic, cycling in Paris remains hazardous.

The Waterways

Today, the Seine and the Paris canal network are used less as working waterways than in previous centuries, although barges still carry some goods along the Seine to the port of Le Havre on the northwest coast. Most river and canal traffic presently consists of pleasure boats. Trips on the Seine, and along canals such as St. Martin's, are among the most popular ways of seeing the sights of Paris.

▼ Heavy rush-hour traffic causes congestion in the city center. This picture shows the area near the Arc de Triomphe with La Grande Arche in the background.

CHAPTER 4

Paris at Work

Paris is at the heart of French trade, business, and industry. Many of Paris's industries developed in the nineteenth century, when industrial development was linked to a rapid expansion of the network of railroads and canals as well as to the growth of the city's population. In the twentieth century, industry began to spread from Paris into the suburbs.

La Défense

La Défense (left) is the new business and residential district on the western outskirts of Paris. Started in 1958, La Défense is probably the most ambitious city planning project undertaken in the Ile de France region. Today, more than 140,000 people work there. La Défense also has housing for more than thirty thousand people, the largest shopping mall in the region, and conference and exhibition facilities. It looks and feels very different from other parts of Paris, with its towering skyscrapers, underground transportation network, and walkways. Many large companies have moved their headquarters there, as office space is bigger and less expensive than in central Paris.

La Grande Arche, built in 1989 in La Défense, has become one of the most distinctive monuments of Paris. Its enormous cube-shaped arch is twice the size of the Arc de Triomphe.

The end of the twentieth century saw major changes in industry and patterns of employment. Most heavy industries moved out to the suburbs or to the new towns in the Ile de France region. Today, much of the economy of the Paris region — especially the city itself — is based on service industries. These are industries such as media, transportation, telecommunications, and tourism that provide a service rather than a manufactured product. About three out of every four working Parisians are now employed in a service industry.

Business and Finance in Paris

Paris's location at the heart of western Europe, its efficient transportation network, its skilled workforce, and its high standard of living have persuaded many leading French and international companies to move there. Paris is the financial center of France and an important center for global finance. The city is the home of the *Bourse*, the French stock exchange, which was established in 1808 by Emperor Napoleon I. Paris is also the headquarters of almost every French bank. The main business districts of Paris center around the Champs Elysées in the 8th arrondissement, the Bourse in the 2nd, and the fashionable 16th arrondissement.

The Fashion Industry

Paris is often regarded as the fashion capital of the world. The fashion industry involves fashion houses and designers, showrooms, designer shops, and design schools. There

▲ *A model struts down the catwalk at the Dior fashion show during Paris Fashion Week in March. This is when major names in fashion show their new designs.*

are also the twice-yearly fashion shows, held at the leading fashion houses, where the best of Paris's designers showcase their latest creations. Few Parisian women can afford these exclusive designs, but the designs often provide the inspiration for cheaper, ready-to-wear clothes.

"Fashion is not something that exists in dresses only. Fashion is in the sky, in the street, fashion has to do with ideas, the way we live, what is happening."

—Coco Chanel, French fashion designer.

33

Tourism in Paris

Paris is the most visited tourist destination in the world, and tourism is a vital part of the city's economy. Thousands of Parisians are employed in the tourist industry, including people who work in hotels, at major tourist attractions, and as tour guides.

Many people who vacation in Paris are drawn by the beauty and romance of the "city of light." But a more recent attraction, both for children and their parents, is the "Magic Kingdom" of Disneyland Paris, which opened in 1992 in Marne-la-Vallée to the east of the city. Paris is also the most popular European destination for business travelers — nearly half of the city's overseas visitors travel there for business meetings, trade fairs, and congresses.

National Government

France is a democratic republic and its government is based in Paris. The country has a president, who serves as head of state and is elected every seven years. France also has a prime minister, who heads the government and comes from the political party with a majority in the National Assembly. Laws are passed by the French Parliament, which is made up of the National Assembly and the Senate. National Assembly members are elected directly in parliamentary elections held every five years. Senators are chosen in a more indirect election and serve for nine years. A third of the senators are re-elected every three years.

Local Government

The Ile de France region has eight administrative units called *départements* (departments), including Paris, its suburbs, and surrounding rural areas. The Ile de France departments are: Hauts-de-Seine, Seine-Saint-Denis, Val-de-Marne, Essonne, Yvelines, Val-d'Oise, Seine-et-Marne, and Paris. The local government of the Ile de France is a regional council made up of 164 members and headed by the regional *préfet* (prefect). Members of the council represent

---

Tourism in Paris

Paris is the world's most popular tourist destination and is especially popular with Americans. In 2002, nearly 2 million Americans visited Paris — nearly 20 percent of all overseas visitors to the city. Next came British tourists (at about 16 percent), then Japanese and Italian tourists (each at about 8 percent).

The main museums and monuments of Paris received 23,500,000 visitors in 2002. The city's top four attractions were:

- *Eiffel Tower: 6,200,000 people*
- *Louvre Museum: 5,700,000 people*
- *Pompidou Center: 5,500,000 people*
- *City of Science and Industry: 2,600,000 people*

Disneyland Paris, which was built in 1992, welcomed 13,100,000 visitors in 2002 and had a total revenue of over 1 billion dollars.

[sources: INSEE/ORTIF; Disneyland Paris Resort]

The city of Paris has a city, or municipal, council and a mayor. The council members meet in the Hôtel de Ville, the town hall of Paris. In addition, each of Paris's twenty arrondissements has its own local council and mayor, with responsibilities for specific local issues, such as housing, services, and environmental concerns.

The Mayor of Paris

The post of mayor of Paris was abolished after the 1871 Paris Commune in an attempt to control the power and the radicalism of the city and its people. The post was reintroduced in 1975 and the first mayoral elections were held in 1977. Paris, like all other French towns and cities, once more had a mayor. The mayor, who is elected and supported by the city council, serves a six-year term and oversees the city's large budget, transportation, economic development, planning, culture, and the environment.

The mayor of Paris holds a powerful post and occupies the third most prominent job in France, after the country's president and prime minister. For years, the city was under the political control of the conservative RPR party, led by Jacques Chirac. In 2001, the city's first socialist mayor, Bertrand Delanoe, was elected.

◀ The impressive Hôtel de Ville (Town Hall) is the home of the city council. The square it overlooks was once a place of public execution, but today, it is the setting for more pleasant forms of public entertainment.

the main political parties of France and are elected every six years. The council has wide-ranging powers in city planning, economic development aid, transportation, the environment, and culture.

35

CHAPTER 5

Paris at Play

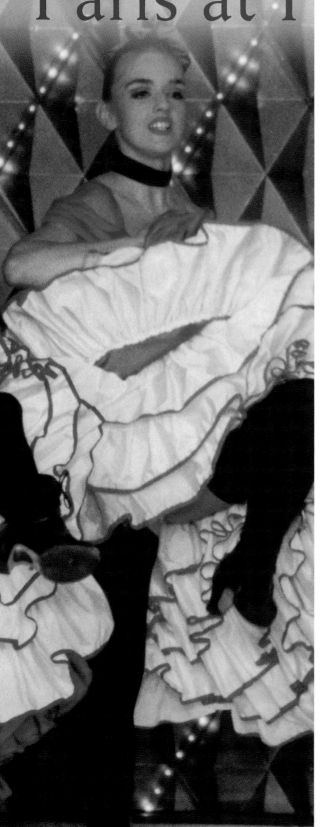

Paris is packed with world-class museums, art galleries, and cultural centers, much loved by Parisians and visitors alike. At night, the city offers a huge variety of entertainment, from the classical and traditional to new and experimental, from grand opera houses to tiny jazz clubs. Parisians can go out for a serious evening of classical theater, or they can spend the night clubbing with the *branché* (the trendy) at one of the city's fashionable clubs or dance venues.

Paris Theater

The most famous theater in Paris is the Comédie Française, where classical tragedies and comedies by great playwrights such as Molière and Racine are performed. The traditional Parisian *cabarets* (nightclubs), such as the Moulin Rouge and the Folies Bergères, are today less popular with Parisians. However, their chorus lines of dancing girls continue to draw large audiences, mostly of tourists. Smaller cabarets and café-theaters offer more intimate settings for listening to *chansons* (French songs) or watching fringe (experimental) theater.

◀ *The cancan, the wild, high-kicking dance that was popularized in the late nineteenth century dance halls of Paris, is still performed in cabaret clubs such as the Moulin Rouge and the Folies Bergères.*

Music

There are concerts of classical music throughout the year, and several of Paris's churches put on regular concerts. The Opéra National performs at the new Opéra de Paris at the Bastille. Opera productions can also be seen at the Opéra Garnier, but since the opening of the Bastille Opéra, it is mainly used for ballet. There are also many venues for rock, pop, and jazz music. Parisians have long been devotees of jazz, and there are dozens of small jazz clubs across the city.

Movies

Parisians are committed moviegoers. The city's many movie theaters show an enormous selection of movies, ranging from *avant-garde* (new and experimental) films to foreign movies, old classics, and the latest Hollywood blockbusters, which are often shown in their original versions, with French subtitles. Although the modern French movie industry has less power and influence than Hollywood, French directors have played a vital part in the development of moviemaking over the last forty years. This is particularly true of the so-called "new wave" French directors of the 1960s and after, such as François Truffaut, Jean-Luc Godard, Alain Resnais, and Louis Malle, who explored new techniques in moviemaking.

Museums and Galleries

The Musée National du Louvre is one of the greatest museums in the world. In recent decades, the museum has undergone several

The Pompidou Center

The Centre Georges Pompidou *(Pompidou Center) was built in the 1970s as part of a major redevelopment plan for the run-down Beaubourg neighborhood. Now an established Paris landmark, this futuristic building (above) shocked many Parisians when the center first opened. The bold and colorful design used a glass and steel framework, with a maze of pipes and escalators placed on the outside. In this way, all the internal space was freed for exhibitions of modern art and for libraries. The center houses the* Musée National d'Art Moderne *(National Museum of Modern Art), an important collection of art from the 1900s to the present day.*

▲ *Intended for demolition in the 1970s, the Gare d'Orsay railroad station was saved by public demand. As the Musée d'Orsay, a museum of nineteenth-century art, it is now one of the city's top attractions.*

Louvre also has masterpieces of European art, including the Mona Lisa, a painting by the great sixteenth-century Italian artist and inventor Leonardo da Vinci.

The Musée d'Orsay is another of Paris's top attractions. Converted from an old railroad station, it contains one of the world's finest collections of nineteenth-century art, with many works by the Impressionists — a group of artists, including Claude Monet and Pierre-Auguste Renoir, who attempted to paint what the eye sees at a particular moment, an "impression," through capturing the ever-changing quality of light. Other popular museums are the *Musée National du Moyen Age* (National Museum of the Middle Ages), with its impressive collection of medieval arts and crafts, and the Musée Carnavalet, the museum of Paris's history.

City of Science and Industry

The City of Science and Industry, opened in 1986, is a complex of museums, theaters, and restaurants that attract millions of visitors each year. Its hands-on science exhibits are very popular with children. Movies are shown on the Géode, a sphere with a gigantic hemispherical screen measuring 118 feet (36 meters) across.

Sporting Paris

Paris hosts many world-class sporting events throughout the year. Many Parisians are passionate about both soccer and rugby. The leading Paris soccer team is Paris St.

modernization projects, including the controversial glass pyramid entranceway. The museum houses antiquities from ancient Egypt, Greece, and Rome, and from the Far East (eastern and southeastern Asia). The

Germain. Its home stadium is at the Parc des Princes. First-division French teams compete there, while international soccer events and rugby are played at the Stade de France in the suburb of Saint-Denis. The stadium, designed as a showcase for French architecture and technology, was opened in 1998 for the soccer World Cup.

Tennis is probably the most popular sport after soccer. The tennis event of the year is the French Open, held in late May and early June at the Roland Garros stadium in the *Bois de Boulogne* (Woods of Boulogne).

There are two major horse-racing tracks in Paris: Longchamp and Auteuil. Every October, Parisians flock to Longchamp in the Bois de Boulogne to watch the Prix de l'Arc de Triomphe, one of the most important races in the world. Some of the finest racehorses compete, cheered on by ardent race goers.

"The heart of each French person beats for the Tour de France."

—Jean-Michel Rochefort of the French Cycling Federation.

The Paris International Marathon takes place in April. Every year, about thirty thousand long-distance runners follow a 26-mile (42-km) course through the heart of the city, starting in the Champs Elysées and ending near the Arc de Triomphe.

Green Paris

Few Parisians have their own yards, so the parks of Paris are much-treasured leisure spots, especially on weekends. In the heart of the city are the Luxembourg Gardens and the Tuileries Gardens where Parisians like to stroll. In the Luxembourg Gardens, people can enjoy playing chess or tennis, or learn

The Tour de France

The 2,000-mile (3,220-km) long Tour de France (left) is the world's lengthiest and toughest cycling race. The route changes every year, but it always ends on the Champs Elysées in Paris, where thousands gather to cheer.

In July 2003, American Lance Armstrong won the Tour for the fifth time in a row, even after overcoming cancer in 1999. Parisians have taken Armstrong to their hearts for his courage and endurance, supporting him as strongly as they do the French riders.

"I will not describe the Bois de Boulogne. It is simply a beautiful, cultivated, endless, wonderful wilderness."

—Mark Twain from *The Innocents Abroad*, 1869.

beekeeping, while children play in the playgrounds or go for pony rides. Another favorite pastime played there and in many other places throughout France is the popular French game of *boules*, in which metal balls are rolled along the ground with the purpose of hitting a smaller wooden ball. Both gardens have elegant layouts, with formal flower beds, fountains, and many statues.

▼ *Children sail model boats in the round pond at the Tuileries Gardens, close to the Louvre Museum.*

In the Latin Quarter is the Jardin des Plantes, botanical gardens established in the seventeenth century by two royal physicians for growing medicinal herbs. Today, it is a leading research center for botany (the science of plants) and is open to the public. People visit to walk in the gardens and enjoy the exotic plants in the greenhouses.

The ancient royal hunting forests of the Bois de Boulogne and Bois de Vincennes were redesigned as parks and were given to the city by Napoleon III in the nineteenth century. Both are vast green areas of more than 2,000 acres (809 hectares) and are extremely popular on weekends for family outings, dog walking, and sports. The Bois de Boulogne, to the west of the city, offers two racecourses, boating on the lake, cycling routes and horseback riding trails. Vincennes to the east has an ancient fortress and a zoo.

▲ *Built by Louis XIV in the seventeenth century, the vast Palace of Versailles became the home of the French court until the French Revolution of 1789.*

Versailles

A popular excursion from Paris is to the magnificent Palace of Versailles and its extensive gardens and parkland, 14 miles (23 km) southwest of the city. The extravagant style of Versailles paints a vivid portrait of the French monarchy in times gone by. Versailles was built on the orders of King Louis XIV, the Sun King. He wanted the most beautiful palace in the world. It took fifty years and more than forty thousand laborers to realize Louis' dreams of perfection. One of the strongest symbols of Louis' power was the bed in the king's bedroom, which was placed at the very heart of the palace. There, each day, the king woke up and went to bed in full view of his royal courtiers, with rituals that recalled the rising and setting of the sun.

The Cemeteries of Paris

The cemeteries of Paris — Père Lachaise, Montmartre, and Montparnasse — are popular tourist spots. Père Lachaise, on the east side of Paris, is reputed to be the most visited cemetery in the world. Many famous people are buried there, including writers such as Molière, Colette, and Oscar Wilde and rock musician Jim Morrison. Part of the cemetery wall is dedicated to the last 147 survivors of the Paris Commune of 1871. They were shot in front of the wall and buried below it in a communal grave.

Looking Forward

Paris, like all world cities, faces major challenges in the twenty-first century. It remains one of the most sophisticated cities in the world, with a strong sense of identity, history, and culture. Yet, it is also a forward-looking city, with ambitious plans for future development.

Population Trends

Population experts have calculated that the number of people living in the Paris metropolitan area will grow significantly by 2015. The suburbs and satellite towns will remain the focus of this population growth, as more lower- and middle-income families move out of the center of Paris, more French people leave rural areas to seek work, and immigrant populations continue to grow. However, the number of people living in the city of Paris is in decline, and a shortage of housing together with rising costs mean this trend is likely to continue.

Redevelopment and Renovation

In recent years, there has been a move away from the "grand projects" of the Mitterrand era. However, there are many plans to redevelop Paris, especially the poorer parts of the city. There are major redevelopment

◄ *The new Seine streetcar line aims to make Paris a healthier environment by helping reduce the number of vehicles on the city's streets.*

plans for the eastern districts of Bercy and Tolbiac, including the new National Library. There are also expansion projects planned in industry and housing for Paris's suburbs and satellite towns. Plans for making the city "greener" are also under way, with the development of new parks and gardens and with tree planting along the Seine.

Dealing with Congestion

Transportation projects are also linked to plans to develop eastern Paris and the suburbs. The city authorities are seeking ways to reduce road traffic, especially on the overcrowded Périphérique. As part of Mayor Delanoe's attempts to make transportation "green," or environmentally friendly, in Paris and to reduce air pollution, there are long-term plans to create a new streetcar line circling the city. In 2003, work began on a streetcar line in the 14th arrondissement. The streetcar system aims to reduce road traffic in the area by 25 percent.

The first part of the Météor, line 14 of the Métro, was opened in 1998. Its driverless, fully automated trains travel at twice the speed of existing Métro trains and have helped to relieve overcrowding on some of the older Métro lines. There are plans to extend the Météor to the southeastern suburbs and to build a new end station in Gennevilliers, to the north of Paris.

Future Prospects

At the beginning of the twenty-first century, many Parisians feel uncertain about the

New Ways of Traveling

As world cities grow larger, planners anticipate major problems in moving large numbers of people over smaller distances. Paris is thinking ahead, with intriguing new transportation ideas that could revolutionize the way people move around big cities. At the main interchange of the Métro in Montparnasse is the new trottoir roulant rapide, *or fast-rolling pavement, which carries passengers at 6 miles (10 km) per hour — about the average speed of a Paris bus.*

Parisians are also being introduced to the American-designed Segway. These chariotlike, two-wheeled scooters are designed for use on pavement and can travel at 12 miles (19 km) per hour. Future plans predict commuters renting Segways to travel to and from Métro stops.

future. They have an aging population: people are living longer and the birthrate is dropping. This will cause problems in the future when there may not be enough people in the workforce to pay for government benefits for those who have retired. Parisians also face problems with unemployment, traffic congestion, and pollution, in addition to the stresses of everyday life in a fast-moving, competitive city. Yet, the essential character of the "city of light" — all the complex elements that make Paris a fascinating, beautiful and unique city — seems secure for many generations to come.

Time Line

c. 250 B.C. Parisii tribe settles on small island in Seine River.

52 B.C. Parisii settlement is conquered by the Romans and is named Lutetia.

Early fifth century A.D. The Roman Empire is in decline; barbarian tribes attack Paris.

508 Frankish leader Clovis makes Paris his capital and founds the Merovingian dynasty.

Eighth century Carolingian dynasty moves capital away from Paris; the city declines.

Tenth–fourteenth centuries Paris grows powerful under the Capetian dynasty and becomes the capital of France.

Fourteenth–fifteenth centuries Under the Valois dynasty, Paris is greatly weakened by the Hundred Years' War.

1348 The Black Death kills thousands of Parisians.

1420–1436 Paris falls under English rule.

Late fifteenth–sixteenth century The Renaissance reaches Paris; the Catholics and Huguenots fight in the Wars of Religion.

1643–1715 The Bourbon king, Louis XIV, reigns; the French court moves to Versailles.

1774–1792 The reign of Louis XVI and his wife, Marie Antoinette, ends in civil unrest.

1789 The storming of the Bastille heralds the beginning of the French Revolution.

1793–1794 The Reign of Terror takes hold of Paris; the monarchy is abolished; the First Republic is declared.

1799 Napoleon Bonaparte seizes power.

1804 Napoleon declares himself Emperor of France; he begins wars of expansion across Europe and centralizes France around Paris.

1815 Napoleon is defeated; the French monarchy is restored.

1820s–1840s The working class grows as the industrial revolution spreads; there are revolutions in 1830 and 1848.

1848–1870 France is made a republic again under Louis-Napoleon, who becomes Emperor Napoleon III; Paris is transformed by Baron Haussmann.

1870–1871 Napoleon III abdicates after war with Prussia; the Paris Commune briefly controls the city until overthrown by the French army.

1871 The Third Republic begins; Paris population continues to grow; Paris begins to modernize.

1914–1918 During World War I, 1 million French soldiers die; the Germans do not quite reach Paris.

1939–1945 During World War II, Paris is occupied by the Germans (1940); Paris is liberated in 1944; Charles de Gaulle becomes president.

1946 De Gaulle resigns; the Fourth Republic begins.

1958 Fifth Republic begins with de Gaulle re-elected as president.

1968 Student and worker unrest; de Gaulle resigns.

1970s and 1980s Pompidou and Mitterrand redevelop and modernize Paris.

1977 Jacques Chirac becomes Mayor of Paris.

1995 and 2002 Chirac is elected president.

Glossary

arrondissements the twenty different districts that make up the city of Paris.

Art Nouveau a style of art and architecture at the end of the nineteenth century. It used curving lines and rich decorations.

asylum-seekers people who leave their own countries because they feel unsafe and are allowed into another country to live.

barbarians agressive and uncivilized people who are usually uneducated and uncultured.

Buddhism a religion based on the teachings of "the Buddha" (the "Enlightened One").

Code Napoleon (or Civil Code) the legal system upon which France's civil laws (especially regarding property, marriage, inheritance, equality before the law, and freedom of religion) are still based.

colony a settlement or country ruled by another, more powerful country.

dynasty a family that rules a country for several generations.

empire a group of different countries ruled by the government of a more powerful country.

the Enlightenment (or the Age of Reason) an approach to religion, politics, and economics, based on progress through rational thinking and science, that greatly influenced aspects of eighteenth-century life in both Europe and America.

fashion houses centers of high fashion, where exclusive clothes are designed and made, usually under the name of one famous designer, for example, Christian Dior.

French Revolution the violent revolution of 1789, which ended the monarchy in France and ushered in a new republic.

grand projects the ambitious and expensive plans of President Mitterrand in the 1980s to build magnificent new buildings in Paris and other regions of France.

guillotine an execution device invented in France that cuts off a person's head with a large blade.

Ile de France an important administrative region in northern France, which includes Paris, its suburbs, and the towns and countryside around Paris.

industrial revolution changes that took place in Europe in the late eighteenth and early nineteenth centuries as a result of the invention of machines capable of producing goods much faster and in much larger quantities than ever before.

Islam a religion based on the life and teachings of the prophet Muhammad, who lived in the seventh century A.D.

Left Bank the part of the city of Paris that is south of the Seine River.

Métro the subway system in Paris.

refugees people who have been forced to flee their own country, often as a result of war or political persecution.

Renaissance a period in European history from the fourteenth to the end of the sixteenth century, characterized by the rediscovery of classical styles from ancient Greece and Rome, the beginnings of modern science, and vigorous artistic activity.

republic a country that is ruled by a head of state or a president, who is elected by the people.

Right Bank the part of the city of Paris that is north of the Seine River.

socialist someone who believes that the community as a whole should control property, industry, and money, and organize them for the good of all.

Further Information

Books
Hoban, Sarah. *Daily Life in Ancient and Modern Paris (Cities Through Time)*. Lerner Publications Company, 2000.

Rawlins, Carol B. *The Seine River (Watts Library: The World of Water)*. Franklin Watts, Inc., 2001.

Rossi, Renzo. *Paris* (first American edition). Enchanted Lion Books, 2003.

Tartaglino, Anna Cazzini. *Medieval Paris (Journey to the Past)*. Raintree/Steck Vaughn, 1997.

Tillier, Alan. *Paris (Eyewitness Travel Guides)*. DK Publishing, 2003.

Web Sites
www.discoverfrance.net/France/Paris/Monuments-Paris/Eiffel.shtml
Discover France pages outlining the history of the Eiffel Tower with links to other Paris monuments.

www.travelforkids.com/Funtodo/France/pariscity/boisdeboulogne.htm
Travel for Kids information on the Bois de Boulogne.

en.wikipedia.org/w/wiki.phtml?title=Louis_XVI_of_France
Wikipedia article on the life of King Louis XVI.

www.frommers.com/destinations/paris/
Frommer's complete guide to the attractions, history, and culture of Paris.

www.kidzworld.com/site/p3662.htm
Information on the storming of the Bastille Prison.

www.un.org/cyberschoolbus/habitat/profiles/paris.asp
United Nations article on the city of Paris.

Index

Page numbers in **bold** indicate pictures.